Just What the Doctor Ordered

(Mind Enhancers)

by

Larry O. Goldbeck, M.D.

ISBN: 1-4033-7780-4 (e-book)
ISBN: 1-4033-7781-2 (Paperback)
ISBN: 1-4033-7782-0 (Hardcover)

Library of Congress Control Number: 2002094652

This book is printed on acid free paper.

Printed in the United States of America
Bloomington, IN

1stBooks – rev. 04/13/04

Rx – For best results use liberally with concentration several times weekly.

Foreword

No apology is made for obvious personal bias in the selection of the 500 "pearls of wisdom" from 250+ eclectic thinkers.

To my wife

Nancy,

my inspiration.

"Some men change their Party for the sake of their principles; others change their principles for the sake of their Party."

Winston Churchill
(1906 General Election)

"It is a mistake to think that misfortunes come from the east or from the west; they originate within one's own mind."

Gautama Buddha

"If I love all faith, so that I can move mountains, and have not love, I am nothing."

Apostle Paul
(Corinthians, 13)

"I protest that if some Great Power would agree to make me always think what is true and do what is right, on condition of being turned into sort of clock and wound up every morning, I think I should instantly close with the offer."

T.H. Huxley

"Gun control advocates resemble the prohibitionists of the 'roaring twenties'. By making liquor illegal, they spawned organized crime, caused bloody violent turf wars and corrupted the criminal justice system. It is the same today with the 'war on drugs'. Prohibition did not stop liquor use; the drug laws can't stop drug use. Making gun ownership illegal will fail too. Criminals will not give up their guns."

David Bergland

"The evil that men do lives after them. The good is oft interred with their bones."

Wm. Shakespeare
(Anthony)

"A thing of beauty is a joy forever; it's loveliness increases; it will never pass into nothingness."

Keats
(Endymion)

"God could not be everywhere and therefore he made mothers."

Anonymous

"I prefer the most unjust peace to the justest war that was ever waged."

Cicero
(Letters to Atticus)

"The Lord prefers common looking people. That is why he made so many of them."

President A. Lincoln

"And 'tis remarkable that they talk most who have the least to say."

Prier
(Alma II)

"Everyone to his taste, as the woman said when she kissed her cow."

Rabelais
(Pantaguel)

"Though I've belted you and flayed you, by the livin' Gawd that made you, you're a better man than I am, Gunga Din."

R. Kipling
(Gunga Din)

"Any fool can make a rule and every fool will mind it."

H. Thoreau

"Government, even in its best state, is but a necessary evil; in its worst state, an intolerable one."

Thomas Paine
(Common Sense)

"Do all the good you can, by all the means you can, in all the ways you can, in all the places you can, at all the times you can, to all the people you can, as long as ever you can."

John Wesley
(His Rule)

"An expert is one who knows more and more about less and less."

N.M. Butler

"God offers to every mind its choice between truth and repose."

R.W. Emerson

"Some Americans need hyphens in their names because only part of them has come over."

President Woodrow Wilson
(1914)

"Grow old along with me! The best is yet to be, the last of life for which the first was made."

R. Browning
(Rabbi Ben Ezra)

3

"The Devil can cite Scripture for his purpose."

Wm. Shakespeare
(Merchant of Venice)

"The conviction of the justification of using even most brutal weapons is always dependent on the presence of a fanatical belief in the necessity of the victory of a revolutionary new order on this globe."

A. Hitler
(Mein Kampf)

"A gentle answer quenches anger and patience is a poultice for all wounds."

Anonymous
(Irish Sayings)

"Cowards die many times before their deaths. The valiant never taste of death but once."

Wm. Shakespeare
(Julius Caesar)

"Relations are simply a tedious pack of people who haven't got the remotest knowledge of how to live nor the smallest instinct about when to die."

Oscar Wilde

"Martyrdom is the only way a man can become famous without ability."

George B. Shaw

"We cry for more police. We protest when the criminal exercises his legal rights for fear he will be set free. We call his legal rights legal loopholes. And in blithe ignorance, to save ourselves from the criminal, we are willing to sacrifice those same constitutional rights that also belong to us."

Attorney Gerry Spence
(Give Me Liberty)

"There is nothing so absurd or ridiculous that has not at some time been said by some philosopher."

Oliver Goldsmith

"Secrecy is not to be measured in altitude. If it were so, many might think the 'Bottom Secret' would be more forceful and suggestive."

Sir Winston Churchill
(at Brendon)

"Our main business is not to see what lies dimly at a distance, but to do what lies clearly at hand."

Carlyle

"What each day needs, that shalt thou ask, each day will set its proper task."

Goethe

"Character is a long standing habit."

Plutarch

"The chief worries of life arise from the foolish habit of looking before and after."

Sir William Osler, MD

"Undress your soul at night not by self examination, but by shedding, as you do your garments, the daily sins whether of omission or of commission, and you will wake a free man with a new life."

George Herbert

"There's a world of capability for joy spread round us, meant for us, inviting us."

Robert Browning

"Realize how much time there is, how long the day is. Realize you have sixteen waking hours, three or four of which at least should be devoted to making a silent conquest of your mental machinery. Concentration is the secret of successful study."

Dr. Osler

"When you love you should not say, 'God is in my heart', but rather, 'I am in the heart of God'. And think not you can direct the course of love, for love, if it finds you worthy, directs your course."

Kahlil Gibran
(The Prophet)

"There is no avoiding damage to character under the Welfare State. Welfare programs cannot help but promote the idea that the government owes the benefits it confers on the individual, and that individual is entitled, by right, to receive them."

Sen. Barry Goldwater
(The Conscience of a Conservative)

"Fortune is fickle."

Dr. Paracelsus

"A man is the architect of his own fortune."

R. Browning

"Those who make peaceful revolution impossible will make violent revolution inevitable."

President J.F. Kennedy

"No one is as hopelessly enslaved as the person who thinks he is free."

Goethe

"The play was a great success but the audience was a failure."

Oscar Wilde

"History is a vision of God's creation on the move."

Arnold Toynbee
(TIME, November 3, 1975)

"The first concern of our law schools is not justice. The words of Oliver Wendall Holmes have become immortalized in the law schools: 'Do not speak to me of justice, young man. This is a court of law.' The failure of lawyers to hear the cry, to listen to the anguish of a people seeking justice, is the principal reason people hold lawyers in such disdain."

Attorney Gerry Spence

"In every family there are times when there is hurt, anger, or alienation. But we cannot run away from our family. We have only family and so, after every falling out, we must make every effort to be reconciled."

Cardinal Joseph Bernardin

"We hold these truths to be self-evident, that all men are created equal, that they are endowed by their Creator with certain inalienable rights; that among these are life, liberty, and the pursuit of happiness."

President Thomas Jefferson
(Declaration of Independence)

"The only purpose for which power can be rightly exercised over any member of civilized community, against his will, is to prevent harm to others. His own good, either physical or moral, is not sufficient warrant. The only part of conduct of any one, for which he is amenable to society, is that which concerns others. In the part which really concerns himself, his independence is, of right, absolute. Over himself, over his own body and mind, the individual is sovereign."

John Stuart Mill

"Inflation is a disease, a dangerous and sometimes fatal disease which if not checked in time can destroy a society. No government is willing to accept responsibility for producing inflation, even in its most virulent degree."

Milton Friedman
(Free to Choose)

"No country in the world is less fitted for a conflict with terrorists than Great Britain, not because of weakness and cowardice, but because of our restraint and our virtues."

Sir Winston Churchill
(House of Commons)

"All the greatest things are simple, and many can be expressed in a single word: Freedom; Justice; Honour; Duty; Mercy; Hope."

Sir Winston Churchill
(1947)

"Something wrong with missionaries – they will save anybody if he is far enough away and don't speak our language."

Will Rogers

"We get smart so late and old so soon."

Anonymous

"There are old pilots and there are bold pilots but very few old <u>and</u> <u>bold</u> pilots."

Eddie Rickenbacker

"To admit that you need something else in life is probably the first step in getting free. It is also to admit that your life has not been as satisfying as you pretend. To waste one's life is to waste the entire world."

David S. Viscott, M.D.
(Feel Free)

"There are five evils in the world. <u>First</u> there is cruelty. <u>Second,</u> there is lack of a clear demarcation between the rights of a father and son; between an elder brother and a younger; between a husband and a wife; between a senior relative and a younger; on every occasion each one desires to be the highest and to profit off the other. They cheat each other; there is deception and a lack of sincerity. <u>Third</u> there is a lack of a clear demarcation as to the behavior between men and women. <u>Fourth,</u> there is a tendency for people to disrespect the rights of others, to exaggerate their own importance at the expense of others, to set bad examples of behavior and, being unjust in their speech, to deceive, slander and abuse others.   Fifth, there is a tendency for people to neglect their duties toward others."

Buddha

"The one charm of marriage is that it makes a life of deception absolutely necessary for both parties."

Oscar Wilde
(Picture of Dorian Gray)

"Don't say:

It can't be done.
We can't afford it.
I'm too tired.
But the children…
We don't have the time.
It's impossible.

Do say:

Sounds great.
How can we swing it?
Let's see how we can possibly do it.
Let's find a way to do it.
Let's think and think until we come up with a solution.

Be a positive thinker."

> Rev. Robert H. Schuller
> (Power Ideas)

"Never give in! Never give in! Never, never, never, never in nothing great or small, large or petty -- never give in except to convictions of honour and good sense."

> Sir Winston Churchill
> (Speech at Harrow School)

"Ah, fill the cup – what boots it to repeat
How time is slipping underneath our feet:
Unborn to-morrow, and dead yesterday,
Why fret about them if to-day be sweet."

> Omar Khayyam
> (The Rubaiyat)

"Why don't they pass a Constitutional Amendment prohibiting anybody from learning anything? And if it works as good as the Prohibition one did, in five years we would have the smartest race of people on earth."

> Will Rogers

"The farther backward you can look, the farther forward you are likely to see."

> Sir Winston Churchill

Larry O. Goldbeck, M. D.

"The moving finger writes; and, having writ, moves on: Nor all thy piety nor wit shall lure it back to cancel half a line, nor all thy tears wash out a word of it."

Omar Khayam
(The Rubaiyat)

"Money and women are the most sought after and the least known about of any two things we have."

Will Rogers

"Many forms of government have been tried and will be tried in this world of sin and woe. No one pretends that democracy is perfect or all wise. Indeed, it has been said that democracy is the worst form of government except all those other forms that have been tried from time to time."

Sir Winston Churchill
(Speech in House of Commons - November 11, 1947)

"I have not yet begun to fight."

Commodore John Paul Jones
(Battling Serapis Aboard Bon Homme Richard, September 23, 1779)

"The seven deadly sins were invented by the Christian Church to insure guilt on the part of the followers. The Christian Church knows that it is impossible for anyone to avoid committing these sins, as they are all things which we, as humans, most naturally do. After inevitably committing these sins financial offerings to the church in order to 'pay off' God are employed as a sop to the parishioner's conscience."

Anton S. La Vey

"Know your lines and don't bump into the furniture."

Spencer Tracy

"Those that want friends to open themselves unto are cannibals of their own hearts."

Francis Bacon
(Of Friendship)

"A good gulp of whiskey at bedtime—it's not very scientific but it helps."

Dr. Alexander Fleming
(Concerning Common Cold)

"America is a great, unwieldy body. Its progress must be slow. It is like a large fleet sailing under convoy. The fleetest sailors must wait for the dullest and slowest."

President John Adams

"Any institutionalized way of thinking eventually must reject the individual who threatens its structure. The obvious conclusion is drawn at the first sign of heresy: What if everyone else followed the example?"

David S. Viscott, M.D.
(Feel Free)

"Duty, Honor, Country. Those three hallowed words reverently dictate what you ought to be, what you can be, what you will be."

Gen. Douglas MacArthur
(May 12, 1962 Address at West Point)

"Short words are best, and the old when short, are the best words of all. This is the sort of English up with which I will not put."

Sir Winston Churchill

"He's one of the few men in the history of this country to run for high office talking out of both sides of his mouth at the same time and lying out of both sides."

Harry S Truman
(Speaking of Nixon)

"Nothing in this life is so exhilarating as being shot at without result."

Sir Winston Churchill

"This war will not end, as the Jews imagine, by the extermination of the European Aryan peoples, but the outcome of this war will be the annihilation of Jewry."

Adolph Hitler
(Speech – January 30, 1942)

"A very dangerous principle is now being established as a social right: Thou shalt not hurt others with words. This principle is a menace—and not just to civil liberties. At the bottom it threatens liberal inquiry—that is, science itself. In English we have a word for the empanelment of tribunals to identify and penalize false and socially dangerous opinions. It is <u>inquisition</u>."

Jonathan Rauch
(Kindly Inquisitors, 1993)

"To utter pleasant words without practicing them, is like a fine flower without fragrance."

Buddha

"Family quarrels are bitter things. They don't go according to any rules. They're not like aches or wounds, they're more like splits in the skin that won't heal because there's not enough material."

F. Scott Fitzgerald

"Let advertisers spend the same amount of money improving their product as they do on advertising and they wouldn't have to advertise it."

Will Rogers

"In war there is no substitute for victory."

Gen. Douglas MacArthur

"Love makes wives and babies, war makes widows and orphans."

> Wm. B. Travis, Lt. Col.
> Army of Texas

"Four score and seven years ago our fathers brought forth on this continent, a new nation, conceived in liberty, and dedicated to the proposition that all men are created equal."

> Abraham Lincoln
> (Gettysburg Address, July 1863)

"Not to be biased is not to be human."

> Jonathan Rauch
> (Kindly Inquisitors)

"Abandon all hope, O ye who enter here."

> Dante
> (Admonition above gates of Hell – DANTE'S INFERNO)

"Let me lay the cards on the table. If I were to give an award for the single best idea anyone has ever had, I'd give it to Darwin, ahead of Newton and Einstein and everyone else. In a single stroke, the idea of evolution by natural selection

unifies the realm of life, meaning, and purpose with the realm of space and time, cause and effect, mechanism and physical law. But it is not just a wonderful idea. It is a dangerous idea."

Daniel Dennett, Philosopher
(From Darwin's Dangerous Idea)

"At its core evolution threatens the sense of specialness we enjoy in a world where we have come to view ourselves as the centerpiece of creation. Its opposite number, opposite creation, is an attractive, appealing, and powerful view. It is also demonstrably, completely, and even tragically wrong."

Professor Kenneth R. Miller
(Finding Darwin's God)

"Build a great character and a great reputation as a wonderful person, and you will be a success."

Rev. Robert H. Schuller
(Power Ideas)

"This has been a most wonderful evening. Gertrude has said things tonight it will take her 10 years to understand."

Alice B. Toklas
(After dinner party with Gertrude Stein)

"Our religious beliefs are many; but one belief is universal with all, and that is that there is some divine being higher than earthly. We can speak to Him in many devious ways, in many languages, but He sees us all in the same light, and judges us according to our actions, as we judge the actions of our children different because we know they are each different."

Will Rogers

"Natural laws and chance may equally be instruments of God's intentions. There can be purpose without an exact predetermined plan."

Ian Barbour
(Physicist and theologian)

"Fascism believes that war alone brings up to its highest tension all human energy

and puts the stamp of nobility upon the people who have the courage to meet it."

Benito Mussolini

"With German officers the French would be a splendid army."

Adolph Hitler

"'Old soldiers never die, they just fade away'. And like the old soldier of that ballad, I now close my military career and just fade away – an old soldier who tried to do his duty as God gave him the light to see that duty. Goodbye."

Gen. Douglas MacArthur
(Speech to Congress, April 19, 1952)

"'Tis a lesson you should heed; try, try, and try again. If at first you don't succeed, try, try, try again."

W.E. Hickson
(Try, Try and Try Again)

"Trifles make perfection, and perfection is no trifle."

Michelangelo
(Quoted by C.C. Colton in Lacon)

"The best-laid schemes o' mice an' men,
Gang aft agley,
An lea'e us nought but quiet and pain,
For promised joy!"

Robert Burns
(To A Mouse)

"Since Auschwitz we know what man is capable of, and since Hiroshima we know what is at stake."

Victor E. Frankel
(Man's Search for Meaning)

"Sed omnia praeclara tam difficilia quam rara sunt", ("but everything great is just as difficult to realize as it is rare to find")

Spinoza
(Ethics)

"I don't think a climb is really worth anything unless you've been scared out of your wits at least twice. If you don't have fear you won't go very high on a mountain. And if you don't learn how to master it, you won't go very high either."

Sir Edmund Hillary
(First man to conquer Mt. Everest)

"My choice of Muhammad to lead the list of the world's most influential persons may surprise some readers and may be questioned by others, but he was the only man in history who was supremely successful on both the religious and secular levels."

Michael H. Hart
(The 100 – A Ranking of the Most Influential Persons in History)

"Nature and nature's law lay hid in night: God said, 'Let Newton be' and all was light."

Alexander Pope

"All that has been accomplished in mathematics since his days has been a deductive, formal and mathematical development of mechanics on the bases of Newton's laws."

Ernst Mach
(Writing in 1901)

"What you do not want done to yourself, do not do to others."

Confucius
(6th Century BC)

"Let the women learn in silence with all subjection. But I suffer not a woman to teach, nor usurp authority over the man, but to be in silence. For Adam was first formed then Eve."

Apostle Paul
(I Timothy 2: 11-13)

"Poverty is the parent of revolution and crime."

Aristotle

"All who have meditated on the art of governing mankind are convinced that the fate of empires depends on the education of youth."

Aristotle

"Martin Luther was not without his faults. He could be extremely intolerant of those who disagreed with him on religious matters. Luther was ferociously anti-Semitic, and the extraordinary viciousness of his writings about the Jews may have helped pave the way for the Hitler ear in the twentieth century in Germany."

Michael H. Hart
(Influential Persons in History)

"The Seljick Turks are occupying the Holy Land, defiling the Christian holy places and molesting Christian pilgrims. All Chrisendom must join together in a holy war, a great crusade to recapture the Holy Land for Christianity. It is fruitful and wealthy. Participation will take the place of all penances and assure the crusader of remission of all his sins."

Pope Urban II
(November 27, 1095 Speech)

"Not a single problem of class struggle has ever been solved in history except by violence."

Vladimir Ilyich Vlynov (Lenin)

"The liberty of man in society is to be under no other legislative power but that established by consent in the commonwealth. There remains still in the people a supreme power to remove or alter the legislative when they find the legislative act contrary to the trust reposed in them.

John Locke
(Two Treatises of Government, 1689)

"The dictatorship of the proletariat is nothing else than power based upon force and limited by nothing—by no law and by absolutely no rule."

Lenin

"I think, therefore I am."

Rene Descartes

"Man is born free; and everywhere he is in chains. The social contract is the total alienation of each associate, and his rights to the whole community."

Jean-Jacques Rousseau

"The natural price of labor is that price which is necessary to enable the laborers, one with another, to subsist and to perpetuate the race, without either increase or diminution."

David Ricardo
(English 19th Century economist and friend of Thomas Malthus)

"Young men are fitter to invent than to judge, fitter for execution than for counsel, and fitter for new projects than for settled business. Men of age object too much, consult too long, adventure too little. Certainly it is good to compound employments of both because the virtues of either age may correct the defects of both."

Francis Bacon
(The Essays, 1597)

"I disapprove of what you say, but I will defend to the death your right to say it."

Francois Marie Arouet (Voltaire)
French apostle of freethinking liberalism

"In taking a state the conqueror must arrange to commit all his cruelties at once, so as not to have to recur to them everyday—benefits should be granted little by little, so that they may be better employed."

Niccolo Machiavelli
(From 'The Prince', 1513)

"Men are so simple and so ready to obey present necessities, that one who deceives will always find those who allow themselves to be deceived."

N. Machiavelli
(From 'The Prince', 1513)

"Heaven sees as the people see; heaven hears as the people hear."

Mencius, Chinese philosopher
(Book of Mencius, about 340 BC)

"Let me be a little kinder,
Let me be a little blinder,
To the faults of those around me."

Edgar A. Guest
('A Creed')

"The truth is incontrovertible. Panic may resent it; ignorance may deride it; malice may destroy it, but there it is."

Sir Winston Churchill
(House of Commons – May 17, 1915)

"There is no king who has not had a slave among his ancestors, and no slave who has not had a king among his."

Helen Keller
(Story of My Life)

Larry O. Goldbeck, M. D.

"He who has a thousand friends has not a friend to spare,
And he who has one enemy shall meet him everywhere."

Omar Khayyam

"My angel—his name is Freedom,
Choose him to be your King;
He shall cut pathways east and west,
And fend you with his wing."

Ralph Waldo Emerson
(Boston Hymn)

"I am not an Athenian nor a Greek, but a citizen of the world."

Socrates
(From Plutarch)

"There is nothing more frightful than ignorance in action."

Johann von Goethe

"The best proof of love is trust."

Dr. Joyce Brothers

"The more laws, the less justice."

Marcus Tullius Cicero De Officiis

"A well regulated militia, being necessary to the security of a free State, the right of

the people to keep and bear Arms, shall not be infringed."

U.S. Constitution, Amendment II

"Among the many misdeeds of the British rule in India, history will look upon the act of depriving a whole nation of arms as the blackest."

Gandhi

This quote refers to the British disarmament of the Indian Army.
Gandhi never advocated the individual using guns.

"Love means never having to say you're sorry."

Erich Segal

"He who has a <u>why</u> to live can bear with almost any <u>how</u>."

Neitzsche

"The penalty for laughing in a courtroom is six months in jail; if it were not for this penalty, the jury would never hear the evidence."

H. L. Mencken

Larry O. Goldbeck, M. D.

"To err is human; to forgive, divine."

Alexander Pope
"An Essay on Criticism"

"To fear love is to fear life, and those who fear life are already three parts dead."

Bertrand Russell

"If you judge people, you have no time to love them."

Mother Theresa

"Some cause happiness wherever they go; others whenever they go."

Oscar Wilde

"Nothing in the world is more dangerous than sincere ignorance and conscientious stupidity."

Martin Luther King, Jr.

"One death is a tragedy. A million deaths is a statistic."

Josef Stalin

"Never attribute to malice that which can be adequately explained by stupidity."

Anonymous

"Nor shall derision prove powerful against those who listen to humanity or those who follow in the footsteps of divinity, for they shall live forever. Forever"

Kahlil Gibran
(The Voice of the Poet)

"Death most resembles a prophet who is without honor in his own land or a poet who is a stranger among his people."

Kahlil Gibran
(The Voice of the Poet)

"You can kill a man but you can't kill an idea."

Medgar Evers

"A man who won't die for something is not fit to live."

Martin Luther King, Jr.

"The report of my death was an exaggeration."

Mark Twain
(After reading his own obituary, June 2, 1897)

29

"Most of the import things in the world have been accomplished by people who have kept on trying when there seemed to be no hope at all."

Dale Carnegie

"A heretic is a man who sees with his own eyes."

Gotthold Ephraim Lessing

"The supreme happiness in life is the conviction that we are loved—loved for ourselves, or rather, loved in spite of ourselves."

Victor Hugo

"Beware how you take away hope from another human being."

Oliver Wendell Holmes

"Hope is a state of mind, not of the world. Hope, in this deep and powerful sense, is not the same as joy that things are going well, or willingness to invest in enterprises that are obviously heading for success, but rather an ability to work for something because it is good."

Vaclav Havel

"Freedom is not worth having if it does not include the freedom to make mistakes."

Mahatma Gandhi

"It is good to shut up sometimes."

Marcel Marceau

"We must use time wisely and forever realize that the time is always ripe to do right."

Nelson Mandela

"When you choose your friends, don't be short-changed by choosing personality over character."

W. Somerset Maugham

"Were it left to me to decide whether we should have a government without newspapers, or newspapers without a

government, I should not hesitate a
moment to prefer the latter."

President Thomas Jefferson
(Letter to Col. Edward Carrington, January 16, 1787)

"The Constitution only gives people the
right to pursue happiness. You have to
catch it yourself."

Ben Franklin

"Read, every day, something no one else is reading. Think, every
day, something no one else is thinking. Do, every day, something no
one else would be silly enough to do. It is bad for the mind to
continually be part of unanimity."

Christopher Morley

"Be courteous to all, but intimate with few, and let those few be well
tried before you give them your confidence. True friendship is a plant
of slow growth, and must undergo and withstand the shocks of
adversity before it is entitled to the appellation."

President George Washington

"A great memory is never made
synonymous with wisdom, any more than
a dictionary would be called a treatise."

John Henry Cardinal Newman
(Oxford University Sermons)

"Don't look a gifthorse in the mouth."

Saint Jerome

"I do not feel obliged to believe that the same God who has endowed us with sense, reason, and intellect has intended us to forgo their use."

Galileo Galilei

"The Lord is my light, and my salvation; whom shall I fear?"

Psalm 27

"Do not go where the path may lead, go instead where there is no path and leave a trail."

Ralph Waldo Emerson

"England and America are two countries separated by the same language."

George Bernard Shaw
(Reader's Digest, November 1942)

"The man who does not read good books has no advantage over the man who cannot read them."

Mark Twain

"He is happiest, be he king or peasant, who finds peace in his home."

Johann von Goethe

"A jury consists of twelve persons chosen to decide who has the better lawyer."

Robert Frost

"Bad habits are like a comfortable bed, easy to get into, but hard to get out of."

Anonymous

"Practice is the best of all instructors."

Publilius Syrus

"Darkness cannot drive out darkness; only light can do that. Hate cannot drive out hate; only love can do that."

Martin Luther King, Jr.

"This is my simple religion. There is no need for temples; no need for complicated philosophy. Our own brain, our own heart is our temple; the philosophy is kindness."

Dalai Lama

"When one door of happiness closes, another opens; but often we look so long at the closed door that we do not see the one which has opened for us."

Helen Keller

"Live free or die."

New Hampshire State Motto

"He who dies with the most toys is, nonetheless, still dead."

Anonymous

"We must respect the other fellow's religion, but only in the sense and to the extent that we respect his theory that his wife is beautiful and his children smart."

H.L. Mencken

"Whenever a separation is made between liberty and justice, neither, in my opinion, is safe."

Edmund Burke

"Character cannot be developed in ease and quiet. Only through experience of trial and suffering can the soul be strengthened, ambition inspired, and success achieved."

Helen Keller

"If you love somebody, let them go. If they return, they were always yours. If they don't, they never were."

Anonymous

"A loving person lives in a loving world. A hostile person lives in a hostile world. Everyone you meet is your mirror."

Ken Keys

"The ultimate measure of a man is not where he stands in moments of comfort, where he stands at times of challenge and controversy."

Martin Luther King, Jr.

"Woe to the man whose heart has not earned while young to hope, to love – and put its trust in life."

Joseph Conrad

"Perfect love is rare indeed – for to be a lover will require that you continually have the subtlety of the very wise, the flexibility of the child, the sensitivity of the artist, the understanding of the philosopher, the acceptance of the saint, the tolerance of the scholar and the fortitude of the certain."

Leo Buscaglia

"Justice delayed is justice denied."

William Gladstone

"The future belongs to those who believe in the beauty of their dreams."

Eleanor Roosevelt

"Those who bring sunshine to the lives of others cannot keep it from themselves."

James Barrie

"Dreams are the touchstones of our character."

Henry David Thoreau

"Forgive your enemies, but never forget their names."

President John Fitzgerald Kennedy

"Question with boldness even the existence of a God; because, if there be one, he must more approve the homage of reason, than that of a blind-folded fear."

President Thomas Jefferson

"Injustice anywhere is a threat to justice everywhere. We are caught in an inescapable network of mutuality, tied in a single garment of destiny. Whatever affects one directly, affects all indirectly."

Martin Luther King, Jr.
(Letter from the Birmingham Jail, April 16, 1963)

"Forgiveness is the answer to the child's dream of a miracle by which what is broken is made whole again, what is soiled is made clean again."

Dag Hammarskjold
Markings, 1964

"To build may have to be the slow and laborious tasks of years. To destroy can be the thoughtless act of a single day."

Sir Winston Churchill

"Human subtlety will never devise an invention more beautiful, more simple or more direct than does Nature, because in her inventions, nothing is lacking and nothing is superfluous."

Leonardo DaVinci

"In three words I can sum up everything I've learned about life: it goes on."

Robert Frost

"Never in the field of human conflict was so much owed by so many to so few."

Sir Winston Churchill

"Genius is one percent inspiration and ninety nine percent perspiration."

Thomas Alva Edison

"The woods are lovely, dark and deep.
But I have promises to keep,
And miles to go before I sleep
And miles to go before I sleep."

Robert Frost
(Stopping by the Woods on a Snowy Evening)

"Imagine the Creator as a stand up comedian – and at once the world becomes explicable."

H.L. Mencken

"Justice is incidental to law and order."

J. Edgar Hoover

"There are more things in heaven and earth, Horatio,
Than are dreamt of in your philosophy."

William Shakespeare
(Hamlet)

Larry O. Goldbeck, M. D.

"In creating, the only hard thing is to begin: a grass blade's no easier to make than an oak."

James Russell Lowell

"If God did not exist, it would be necessary to invent Him."

Voltaire

"It is better that ten guilty escape than one innocent suffer."

William Blackstone

"Two roads diverged in a wood and I – I took the one less travelled by, and that has made all the difference."

Robert Frost

"I have a dream, that my four little children will one day live in a nation where they will not be judged by the color of their skin but by the content of their character. I have a dream today!"

Martin Luther King, Jr.

"Choose your friends by their character and your socks by their color. Choosing your socks by their character makes no sense, and choosing your friends by their color is unthinkable."

Anonymous

"No man is ever old enough to know better."

Holbrook Jackson
(Ladies Home Journal – January 1950)

"A woman's always younger than a man of equal years."

Elizabeth Barrett Browning
(Aurora Leigh)

"We are all born for love. It is the principle of existence, and its only end."

Benjamin Disraeli

"So long as we have enough people in this country willing to fight for their rights, we'll be called a democracy."

Roger Baldwin

"An insincere and evil friend is more to be feared than a wild beast; a wild beast may wound your body, but an evil friend will wound your mind."

Buddha

"The only way to have a friend is to be one."

Ralph Waldo Emerson

"…happiness is the highest good, being a realization and perfect practice of virtue, which some can attain, while others have little or none of it…"

Aristotle

"The sweetest of all sounds is praise."

Xenophon

"Always when I see a man fond of praise I always think it is because he is an affectionate man craving for affection."

J.B. Yeats
(Letters to His Son, W.B. Yeats and Others)

"Courage is the price that life exacts for granting peace."

Amelia Earhart

"In a democracy dissent is an act of faith. Like medicine, the test of its value is not in its taste, but in its effects."

J.W. Fulbright

"Many an opportunity is lost because a man is out looking for four-leaf clovers."

Anonymous

"Every good communist should know that political power grows out of the barrel of a gun."

Mao Tse Tung

"Opportunity may knock only once, but temptation leans on the doorbell."

Anonymous

"The fearless are merely fearless. People who act in spite of their fear are truly brave."

James A. LaFond-Lewis
November 11, 1999

"He who does not have the courage to speak up for his rights cannot earn the respect of others."

René G. Torres

"Be happy while you're living, for you're a long time dead."

Scottish Proverb

"Quemadmodum gladius Neminem occidit, occidentis telum est." (A sword never kills anybody; it is a tool in the killer's hand.)

Seneca
(Letters to Lucilius)

"Opportunities are usually disguised as hard work, so most people don't recognize them."

Ann Landers

"Immature love says: 'I love you because I need you.' Mature love says 'I need you because I love you.'"

Erick Fromm

"The grand essentials of happiness are: something to do, something to love, and something to hope for."

Allan K. Chalmers

"Scratch a Russian and you'll find a Tartar."

Napoleon

"For it was not into my ear you whispered, but into my heart. It was not my lips you kissed, but my soul."

Judy Garland

"The strongest reason for the people to retain the right to keep and bear arms is, as a last resort, to protect themselves against tyranny in government."

Thomas Jefferson

"Where there is love there is life."

Mahatma Gandhi

"Self-sacrifice enables us to sacrifice other people without blushing."

Bernard Shaw
(Maxims for Revolutionists)

"Blessings on him that first invented sleep."

Cervantes
(Don Quixote, II)

"There is but one step from the sublime to the ridiculous."

Napoleon

"All they that shall take the sword shall perish with the sword."

New Testament
(Mathew XXVI, 52)

"A teacher affects eternity; one can never tell where the influence stops."

Henry Adams

"Yond Cassius has a lean and hungry look; he thinks too much: such men are dangerous."

Shakespeare
(Julius Caesar, 1,2)

"'They are fools who kiss and tell'
Wisely has the poet sung.
Man may hold all sorts of posts
If he'll only hold his tongue."

R. Kipling
(Pink Dominoes)

"Ye shall know the truth, and the truth shall make ye free."

New Testament
(John, VIII, 13)

"Resistance to tyrants is obedience to God."

Thomas Jefferson
(Epigrams)

"Virtue is its own reward."

Cicero
(De finibus)

"They also serve who only stand and wait."

Milton
(Sonnet; On His Blindness)

"Wives are young men's mistresses, companions for middle age, and old men's mistresses."

Francis Bacon
(Essays of Marriage and Single Life)

"I only regret that I have but one life to lose for my country."

Nathan Hale
(Speech before his execution, September 22, 1776)

"Religion is the opium of the people."

Karl Marx

"My candle burns at both ends;
It will not last the night;
But, oh, my foes, and oh, my friends –
It gives a lovely light."

Edna St. Vincent Millay
(A Few Figs for Thistles)

"Verily I say unto you, inasmuch as ye have done It unto one of the least of these my brethren, ye have done it unto me."

Jesus Christ
(Mathew XXV, 40)

"This generation of Americans has a rendezvous with destiny."

President Franklin D. Roosevelt
(Speech, 1936)

"The only thing we have to fear is fear itself."

FDR
(First Inaugural Address, 1933)

"Fortune favors the bold."

Virgil
(Aeneid X)

"One small step for man; one giant step for mankind."

Neil Armstrong
(First moon landing, 1969)

"We have met the enemy and him is us."

Pogo
(Comic strip by Kelley)

"I'll worry about that tomorrow."

Scarlett O'Hara
(Gone with the Wind by Mitchell)

"War is hell."

Gen. Tecumseh Sherman

"Get there firstus with the mostus."

Gen. Nathan Bedford Forest
(Explanation of how to win a battle, 1863)

"Frankly, Scarlett, I don't give a damn."

Rhett Butler
(Gone with the Wind by Mitchell)

"A billion here and a billion there and before long, gentlemen, we are talking <u>real</u> <u>money</u>."

Senator Everett Dirksen
(Speech to Congress)

"Mr. Gorbachav, tear down that wall."

President Ronald Reagan

"I never met a man I didn't like."

Will Rogers

Larry O. Goldbeck, M. D.

"The buck stops here."

President Harry Truman

"The more people I meet the more I love my golden retriever, HoneySue."

Dr. Larry O. Goldbeck

"People dig their graves with their teeth. They eat three meals a day. One is for themselves, one is for the doctors, and one is for the undertakers."

Eugene O. Goldbeck

"The stock market has bears, bulls and pigs and the latter often become slaughtered."

Anonymous

"Property is surely a right of mankind as real as liberty. The moment the idea is admitted into society that property is not sacred as the laws of God, and that there is not a force of law and public justice to

50

protect it, anarchy and tyranny commence."

President John Adams

"In my view, a drug "war" has been perverted too often into a series of frontal attacks on basic American constitutional guarantees – including due process, the presumption of innocence, and the right to own and enjoy private property. Foremost among the invasions we now witness are unrelenting government assaults on property rights, fueled by a dangerous and emotional vigilante mentality that sanctions shredding the U.S. Constitution into meaningless confetti."

Representative Henry Hyde
(Protecting our Property Rights)

"The woods are full of long drivers."

Golf Coach, Harvey Penick
(Little Red Book)

"Indecision is a killer."

> Harvey Penick
> (Golf Coach)

"My ancestors didn't come over on the Mayflower, but they met the boat."

> Will Rogers

"Consider the past and you will know the future."

> Old Chinese Proverb

"The publicans and the harlots go into the kingdom of God before you."

> Jesus Christ
> (Speaking to the Pharasees)

"Man can cure disease but not fate."

> Old Chinese Proverb

"Things in our country run in spite of the government; not by aid of it."

> Will Rogers

"I love a dog. He does nothing for political reasons."

> Will Rogers

"Learning is like rowing upstream; not to advance is to drop back."

> Old Chinese Proverb

"We have the best politicians money can buy."

Will Rogers

"I'm not as much interested in the men in my life as I am the life in my men."

Mae West

"If I had known I would live so long, I would have taken better care of myself."

Groucho Marx

"I attribute some of my longevity to helping ladies across the street – often to my place."

George Burns

"We will not tire; we will not falter; we will not fail."

President George W. Bush

"I am not a crook."

President Richard Nixon

"Speak softly but always carry a big stick; you will go far."

President Theodore Roosevelt, 1901

"I am afraid we have awakened a sleeping giant."

Admiral Yamato Isoruku
(After Pearl Harbor, December 7, 1941)

"When you are older, my son, you will understand that for every man there comes a time to love and a time to die. You are living proof that I have loved, and I will meet my other commitment with honor. In this world nothing is forever – not life, nor death, not poverty, nor riches, not tyranny that I fight, nor the liberty for which I die. Nothing is forever."

William Barret Travis, Lt. Col.
Commander of the Alamo
(Last letter to his son)

"In war there is no substitute for victory."

General Douglas MacArthur

"Damn the torpedoes."

Admiral David Farragut
Mobile Bay, August 5, 1864

"December 7, 1941, was a day that will live in infamy."

President Franklin Roosevelt
(Speech to Congress, December 8, 1941)

"Destiny is not a matter of chance, it is a matter of choice; it is not a thing to be waited for, it is a thing to be achieved."

William Jennings Byran

"The only thing necessary for the triumph of evil is for good men to do nothing."

Edmund Burke

"The price of greatness is responsibility."

Sir Winston Churchill

"It is an old maxim of mine that when you have excluded the impossible, whatever remains, however improbable, must be the truth."

Conan Doyle
(The Adventures of Sherlock Holmes – "The Beryl Coronet")

"Education is the ability to listen to almost anything without losing your temper or your self-confidence."

Robert Frost

"The revolution...is a dictatorship of the exploited against the exploiters."

Fidel Castro

"The foundation of every state is the education of its children."

Diogenes

"It was the best of times, it was the worst of times."

Charles Dickens
(A Tale of Two Cities)

"Music is well said to be the speech of angels."

Thomas Carlyle

"The inherent vice of capitalism is the unequal sharing of blessings; the inherent virtue of socialism is the equal sharing of miseries."

Sir Winston Churchill

"Time is money."

Benjamin Franklin
(Advice to a Young Tradesman)

"When making a decision of minor importance, I have always found it advantageous to consider all the pros and cons. In vital matters, however, such as the choice of a mate or a profession, the decision should come from the unconscious, from somewhere within ourselves. In the important decisions of personal life, we should be governed, I think, by the deep inner needs of our nature."

Sigmund Freud

"Leadership is the art of getting someone else to do something you want done because he wants to do it."

Dwight D. Eisenhower

"He that falls in love with himself will have no rivals."

Benjamin Franklin

"The test of a first-rate intelligence is the ability to hold two opposed ideas in mind at the same time and still retain the ability to function."

F. Scott Fitzgerald

"At last is Hector stretch'd upon the plain,
Who fear'd no vengeance for Patroclus slain:
Then, Prince! You should have fear'd, what now you
Achilles absent was Achilles still:
Yet a short space the great avenger stayed,
Then low in dust thy strength and glory laid."

Homer
(The Iliad)

"I hate facts. I always say the chief end of man is form general propositions – adding that no general proposition is worth a damn."

Oliver Wendell Holmes, Jr.
(The Mind and Faith of Justice Holmes)

"Obstacles are those frightful things you see when you take your eyes off your goal."

Henry Ford

"We do not have to visit a madhouse to find disordered minds; our planet is the mental institution of the universe."

Johann von Goethe

"Extremism in the defense of liberty is no vice. And moderation in the pursuit of justice is no virtue."

Barry Goldwater

"Avarice, envy, pride,
Three fatal sparks, have set the hearts of all
On Fire."

Dante Alighieri
(The Divine Comedy)

"It is better to be violent, if there is violence in our hearts, than to put on the cloak of nonviolence to cover impotence."

Mahatma Gandhi

"A well-trained dog will make no attempt to share your lunch. He will just make you feel so guilty that you cannot enjoy it."

Helen Thomson

"It's kind of fun to do the impossible."

Walt Disney

"A dog is the only thing on this earth that loves you more than he loves himself."

Josh Billings
(Henry Wheeler Shaw)

"No one appreciates the very special genius of your conversation as a dog does."

Christopher Morley

"If you don't like something, change it. If you can't change it, change your attitude. Don't complain."

Maya Angelou

"You can't build a reputation on what you're going to do."

Henry Ford

"We shall defend our island, whatever the cost may be, we shall fight on the beaches, we shall fight on the landing grounds, we shall fight in the fields and in the streets, we shall fight in the hills; we shall never surrender."

Sir Winston Churchill

"When I'm working on a problem, I never think about beauty. I think only how to solve the problem. But when I have finished, if the solution is not beautiful, I know it is wrong."

Richard Buckminster Fuller

"Knowing is not enough; we must apply. Willing is not enough; we must do."

Johann von Goethe

"Live as if you were to die tomorrow. Learn as if you were to live forever."

Mahatma Gandhi

"They never fail who die in a great cause."

George Gordon Byron

"Don't try to buy at the bottom and sell at the top. It can't be done except by liars."

Bernard Baruch

"I made my money by selling too soon."

Bernard Baruch

"Time goes by so fast, people go in and out of your life. You must never miss the opportunity to tell these people how much they mean to you."

"Cheers"

"Friendship is the hardest thing in the world to explain. It's not something you learn in school. But if you haven't learned the meaning of friendship, you really haven't learned anything."

Muhammad Ali

"For many are called, but few are chosen."

Matthew 22:14

"Experience should teach us to be most on our guard to protect liberty when the government's purposes are beneficial. The greatest dangers to liberty lurk in insidious encroachment by men of zeal, well meaning but without understanding."

Louis D. Brandeis

"For an actress to be a success, she must have the face of a Venus, the brains of a Minerva, the grace of Terpsichore, the memory of a MaCaulay, the figure of Juno, and the hide of a rhinoceros."

Ethel Barrymore

"A kiss is a lovely trick designed by nature to stop speech when words become superfluous."

Ingrid Bergman

"Adversity is the first path to truth."

George Gordon Byron
(Don Juan)

"The beauty of religious mania is that it has the power to explain everything. Once God (or Satan) is accepted as the first cause of everything which happens in the mortal world, nothing is left to chance...logic can be happily tossed out the window."

Stephen King

"Our progress as a nation can be no swifter than our progress in education. The human mind is our fundamental resource."

John Fitzgerald Kennedy

"People are just as happy as they make up their minds to be."

Abraham Lincoln

"Most people give up just when they're about to achieve success. They quit on the one-yard line. They give up at the last minute of the game one foot from a winning touchdown."

H. Ross Perot

"There is much pleasure to be gained from useless knowledge."

Bertrand Russell

"You can fool some of the people some of the time and all of the people some of the time, but you can't fool all of the people all of the time."

Abraham Lincoln

"A doctor can bury his mistakes but an architect can only advise his client to plant vines."

Frank Lloyd Wright

"Words are, of course, the most powerful drug used by mankind."

Rudyard Kipling

"It requires wisdom to understand wisdom: the music is nothing if the audience is deaf."

Walter Lippman

"No pessimist ever discovered the secret of the stars, or sailed to an uncharted land, or opened a new doorway for the human spirit."

Helen Keller

"We must learn to live together as brothers or perish together as fools."

Martin Luther King, Jr.

"An invasion of armies can be resisted, but not an idea whose time has come."

Victor Hugo

"I felt invincible. My strength was that of a giant. God was certainly standing by me. I smashed five saloons with rocks before I ever took a hatchet."

Carry Nation

"Nothing happens by itself...it all will come your way, once you understand that you have to make it come your way, by your own exertions."

Ben Stein

"As I would not be a slave, so I would not be a master. This expresses my idea of democracy."

Abraham Lincoln

"He conquers who endures."

Persius

"Ask not what your country can do for you; ask what you can do for your country."

John Fitzgerald Kennedy
(Inaugural Address)

"Let your hook be always cast. In the pool where you least expect it, will be fish."

Ovid

"The best minds are not in government. If any were, business would steal them away."

Ronald Reagan

"You must do the things you think you cannot do."

Eleanor Roosevelt

"The goal of education is the advancement of knowledge and the dissemination of truth."

John Fitzgerald Kennedy

"It is not fair to ask of others what you are not willing to do yourself."

Eleanor Roosevelt

"Being deeply loved by someone gives you strength; loving someone deeply gives you courage."

Lao-Tzu

"When you are content to be simply yourself and don't compare or compete, everybody will respect you."

Lao-Tzu

"The taxpayer – that's someone who works for the federal government but doesn't have to take the civil service examination."

President Ronald Reagan

"Never look down on anybody unless you are helping him up."

Jesse Jackson

"We cannot change anything until we accept it. Condemnation does not liberate, it oppresses."

C.G. Jung
(Psychological Reflections)

"It is an old habit with theologians to beat the living with the bones of the dead."

Robert G. Ingersoll

"Life becomes harder for us when we live for others, but it also becomes richer and happier."

Albert Schweitzer, M.D.

"You shall know the truth, and the truth shall make you mad."

Aldous Huxley

"That government is best which governs the least, because its people discipline themselves."

President Thomas Jefferson

"From each, according to his ability; to each, according to his need."

Karl Marx

"I think that I shall never see
A poem as lovely as a tree."

Joyce Kilmer
(Trees)

"Wealth is the product of man's capacity to think."

Ayn Rand

"I find that the harder I work, the more luck I seem to have."

President Thomas Jefferson

"I'm fed up to the ears with old men dreaming up wars for young men to die in."

Senator George McGovern

"What would not I give to wander
Where my old companions dwell?
Absence makes the heart grow fonder,
Isle of Beauty, fare thee well!"

John Milton
(Paradise Lost)

"So you think that money is the root of all evil. Have you ever asked what is the root of all money?"

Ayn Rand

"One of the penalties for refusing to participate in politics is that you end up being governed by your inferiors."

Plato

"You can tell whether a man is clever by his answers. You can tell whether a man is wise by his questions."

Naguib, Mahfouz

"She would rather light candles than curse the darkness and her glow has warmed the world."

Senator Adlai Stevenson
`(Eulogy of Eleanor Roosevelt, November 7, 1962)

"To cease smoking is the easiest thing I ever did. I ought to know, I've done it a thousand times."

Mark Twain

"Power is the ultimate aphrodisiac."

Henry Kissinger

"Happiness lies in the joy of achievement and the thrill of creative effort."

President Franklin Roosevelt

"Do what you can, with what you have, where you are."

President Theodore Roosevelt

"Few things can help an individual more than to place responsibility on him, and to let him know that you trust him."

Booker T. Washington
(Up From Slavery)

"A wise man is superior to any insults which can be put upon him, and the best reply to unseemly behavior is patience and moderation."

Moliére
(The Would-be Gentleman)

"It is easier to find men who will volunteer to die, than to find those who are willing to endure pain with patience."

Julius Caesar

"There is not greater love than this: to lay down one's life for one's friends."

Jesus Christ
(John 15:13)

"Freedom is first of all one's birthright. What does a person owe the government other than to making an honest living and minding his own business? When government decides you owe it something, that obligation is encoded into law. The right to compel you by physical force, usually called police power, is what makes government different from all other human institutions. An adult making an honest living and minding his own business deserves to be left alone to live his life as he chooses. He deserves to be free."

Charles Murray
(What It Means to be a Libertarian)

"From Watergate we learned what generations before us have known; our Constitution works. And during Watergate years it was interpreted again so as to reaffirm that no one – absolutely no one – is above the law."

Leon Jaworski

"Guard with jealous attention the public liberty. Suspect everyone who approaches that jewel. Unfortunately, nothing will preserve it but downright force. Whenever you give up that force, you are inevitably ruined."

Patrick Henry

"Never believe that a few caring people can't change the world. For, indeed, that's all who ever have."

Margaret Mead

"Never believe that a man is telling the truth when you know that you would lie if you were in his place."

H. L. Mencken

"The function of socialism is to raise suffering to a higher level."

Norman Mailer

"A lie told often enough becomes truth."

Lenin (Vladimir Ulyanov)

"Money is like manure. You have to spread it around or it smells."

J. Paul Getty

Larry O. Goldbeck, M. D.

"Is life so dear or peace so sweet as to be purchased at the price of chains and slavery? Forbid it, Almighty God! I know not what course others may take, but as for me, give me liberty, or give me death!"

Patrick Henry

"Facts do not cease to exist because they are ignored."

Aldous Huxley

"Ye have the poor with you always."

Jesus
(Mark 14:7)

"Discrimination has become a synonym for racial bigotry. This perverts an honorable concept. To discriminate is to perceive differences. To perceive differences often means to think that one thing is better than another in some way. In a <u>free</u> society freedom of association cannot be abridged. Implicit in this freedom is also the freedom <u>not</u> to associate."

Charles Murray
(What It Means to be a Libertarian)

"I believe most Americans do not realize the grave extent to which our constitutional protections have been violated and diminished in recent years."

Henry Hyde, U.S. Representative
(from Forfeiting Our Property Rights)

"Fear of punishment never made man truly honest. Moral courage is requisite to meet the wrong and proclaim the right."

Mary Baker Eddy
(from Science and Health)

"In politics, nothing happens by accident. If it happens, you can bet it was planned that way."

President Franklin Roosevelt

"Government doesn't work and so it isn't to government that we should look for remedies."

Harry Browne
Economist

"Every puppy should have a boy."

Erma Bombeck

"For by the words thou shalt be justified, and by thy words thou shalt be condemned."

Jesus
(Mathew 12:37)

"The quiet life in day-tight compartments will help you to bear your own and others' burdens with a light heart. Life is a straight and plain business.

Sir William Osler
(A Way of Life)

"Your children are not your children. Though they are with you, they belong not to you. You may give them your love but not your thoughts. You may house their bodies but not their souls. For their souls dwell in the house of tomorrow, which a parent can't visit, not even in a wildest dream."

Kahlil Gibran

"The word Christ is not properly a synonym for Jesus, though it is commonly so used. Jesus was a human name, which belonged to him in common with other Hebrew boys and men, for it is identical with the name Joshua, the renowned Hebrew Leader. On the other hand, Christ is not a name so much as the divine title of Jesus, synonymous with Messiah."

Mary Baker Eddy

"The powers not delegated to the United States by the constitution, nor prohibited by it to the States, are reserved to the States respectively, or to the people."

U.S. Constitution
10th Amendment, December 15, 1791

"I never travel without my diary. One should always have something sensational to read in the train.

Oscar Wilde
(The Importance of Being Earnest)

"Two months prior to the passage of the Federal Reserve Act, a mechanism to collect funds to pay interest on the national debt was created. That mechanism was the progressive income tax, the second plank of Karl Marx's Communist Manifesto which contained these planks for "socializing" a country."

Senator Barry Goldwater
(None Dare Call It Conspiracy)

"I believe, as did St. Thomas Aquinas, and Aristotle before him, that natural law recognizes in every person the right to property."

Henry Hyde, U.S. Representative
(from Forfeiting Our Property Rights)

"You must live with a person to know a person."

Old Irish Saying
"Oh, what a tangled web we weave,
When first we practice to deceive."

Sir Walter Scott
(Marmion)

"It is better to die on your feet than to live on your knees."

Emiliano Zapata

"If you tell the truth, you don't have to remember anything."

Mark Twain

"Power always has to be kept in check; power exercised in secret, especially under the cloak of national security, is doubly dangerous."

Senator William Proxmire

"Whenever you find yourself on the side of the majority, it's time to pause and reflect."

Mark Twain

"Somewhere, something incredible is waiting to be known."

Dr. Carl Sagan

"Illegitimis non carborundum." (Lat. – "Don't let the bastards grind you down.")

Gen. Joseph Stilwell

"Communism is the corruption of a dream of justice."

Senator Adlai Stevenson

"Peace is not an absence of war, it is a virtue, a state of mind, a disposition for benevolence, confidence, justice."

Baruch Spinoza

"When you get to the end of your rope, tie a knot and hang on."

President Franklin D. Roosevelt

"No one can make you feel inferior without your consent."

Eleanor Roosevelt

"The best defense against usurpatory government is an assertive citizenry."

William F. Buckley, Jr.

"All adventure is now reactionary."

William F. Buckley, Jr.

"Intellectual freedom is the only guarantee of a scientific democratic approach to politics, economic development and culture."

Andrei D. Sakharov

"All truth passes through three stages: first it is ridiculed, second it is violently opposed, third it is accepted as being self-evident."

Arthur Schopenhauer

"I would have made a good pope."

President Richard M. Nixon

"A woman can never be too rich or too thin."

Wallis, Duchess of Windsor

"Fill what's empty, empty what's full and scratch where it itches – my secret for a long and happy life."

Wallis, Duchess of Windsor

"First they ignore you, then laugh at you; then they fight you; then you win."

Mahatma Gandhi

"A narcissist is someone better looking than you are."

Gore Vidal

"Some people ask the secret of our long marriage. We take time to go to a good restaurant two times a week. A little candlelight, dinner, soft music and dancing. She goes Tuesdays, I go Fridays."

Henny Youngman

"I wouldn't be caught dead marrying a woman old enough to be my wife."

Tony Curtis

"The appropriate age for marriage is around eighteen for girls and thirty-seven for men."

Aristotle

"Do not trust to the cheering, for those persons would shout as much if you and I were going to be hanged."

Oliver Cromwell

"Dictionary is the only place that success comes before work. Hard work is the price we must pay for success. I think you can accomplish anything if you're willing to pay the price."

Vince Lombardi

"If I have seen further it is because I have stood on the shoulders of giants."

Sir Isaac Newton

"Love is temporary insanity curable by marriage."

Ambrose Bierce

"She looks as if she'd been poured into her clothes and had forgotten to say when."

P.G. Wodehouse

"Men should be like Kleenex: soft, warm and disposable."

Cher

"If you've got them by the balls, their hearts and minds will follow."

John Wayne

"It's better to be black than gay because when you're black you don't have to tell your mother."

Charles Pierce

"Life is a sexually transmitted disease, and the mortality rate is one hundred percent."

R.D. Lang

"Sex without love is an empty experience, but as empty experiences go, it's a pretty good one."

Woody Allen

"Once you learn to quit, it becomes a habit."

Vince Lombardi

"For what is done or learned by one class of women becomes, by virtue of their common womanhood, the property of all women."

Elizabeth Blackwell, MD
First woman to become a doctor in the United States

"I am so anxious for you not to abdicate and I think the fact that you do is going to put me in the wrong light to the entire world because they will say that I could have prevented it."

Wallis, Duchess of Windsor

"In war, events of importance are the result of trivial causes."

Julius Caesar

"It may seem a strange principle to enunciate as the very first requirement in a hospital that it should do the sick no harm."

Florence Nightingale, 1859

"All right Mister, let me tell you what winning means…you're willing to go longer, work harder, give more than anyone else."

Vince Lombardi

"Far away there in the sunshine are my highest aspirations. I may not reach them, but I can look up and see their beauty, believe in them, and try to follow where they lead."

Louisa May Alcott

"Ninety-nine percent of the failures come from people who have the habit of making excuses."

Dr. George Washington Carver

"I am also very proud to be a liberal. Why is that so terrible these days? The liberals were liberators – they fought slavery, fought for women to have the right to vote, fought against Hitler, Stalin, fought to end segregation, fought to end apartheid. Liberals put an end to child labor and they gave us the five-day workweek! What's to be ashamed of?"

Barbra Streisand

"I found that when I talk to the little flower or to the little peanut they will give up their secrets…"

"Nature is an unlimited broadcasting station, through which God speaks to us every hour, if we only will tune in."

Dr. George Washington Carver

"The family unit plays a critical role in our society and in the training of the generation to come."

Sandra Day O'Connor
Supreme Court Justice

"If we are to achieve a richer culture, rich in contrasting values, we must recognize the whole gamut of human potentialities, and so weave a less arbitrary social fabric, one in which each diverse gift will find a fitting place."

Margaret Mead

"Son, be of good cheer, thy sins are forgiven."

Jesus Christ

"Cautious, careful people always casting about to preserve their reputation or social standards never can bring about reform. Those who are really in earnest are willing to be anything or nothing in the world's estimation, and publicly and privately, in season and out, avow their sympathies with despised ideas and their advocates, and bear the consequences."

Susan B. Anthony

"The devil does not sleep."

Martin Luther

"The day will come when men will recognize woman as his peer, not only at the fireside, but in councils of the nation. Then, and not until then, will there be the perfect comradeship, the ideal union between the sexes that shall result in the highest development of the race."

Susan B. Anthony

"A companion loves some agreeable qualities which a man may possess, but a friend loves the man himself."

James Boswell

"And the wave of her hand stays the Angel of Death;
She nurses him back and restores once again
To both army and state the brave leader of men.
She has smoothed his black plumes and laid them to sleep,
Whilst the angels above them their high vigils keep:
And she sits here alone, with the snow on her brow
Your cheers for her comrades! Three cheers for her now.
And these were the women who went to the war."

Nurse Clara Barton
(The Women Who Went to the Field)

"Verily the <u>true</u> religion in the sight of God is Islam. And fight for the religion of God against those who fight against you, but transgress not by attacking them first, for God loveth not the transgressors. And kill them whenever ye find them, and turn them out of that whereof they have disposed you; for temptation to idolotry is more grievous than slaughter."

Mohammed
(Koran)

"He who joyfully marches to music, rank and file, has already earned my contempt."

Albert Einstein

"Saving is a very fine thing. Especially when your parents have done it for you."

Winston Churchill

"A sympathetic friend can be quite as dear as a brother."

Homer

"Pray while you're well, because if you wait until you're sick you might not be able to do it."

Joseph Cardinal Bernardin

"My religion consists of a humble admiration of the illimitable superior spirit who reveals himself in the slight details we are able to perceive with our frail and feeble mind."

Albert Einstein

"A friend is a present you give yourself."

Robert Louis Stevenson

"And Moses said. "When the Lord gives you meat to eat in the evening and your fill of bread in the morning, because the Lord has heard the complaining that you utter against him-what are we! Your complaining is not against us but against the Lord."

Moses
To the Israelites

"13. But Moses said to God, "If I come to the Israelites and say to them, 'The God of your ancestors has sent me to you,' and they ask me, 'What is his name?' what shall I say to them?" 14. God said to Moses, "I AM WHO I AM." He said further, "Thus you shall say to the Israelites, I AM has sent me to you.'" 15. God also said to Moses, "thus you shall say to the Israelites, 'The Lord, the God of your ancestors, the God of Abraham, the God of Isaac, and the God of Jacob, has sent me to you.'"

Moses
(Exodus)

"Sometimes one pays most for the things one gets for nothing."

"Science without religion is lame. Religion without science is blind."

"Imagination is more important than knowledge."

Albert Einstein

"Most Excellent Leo, I beseech you to accept my vindication made in this letter. I have no dispute with any man concerning morals, but only concerning the word of truth. I neither can nor will forsake and deny the word."

Martin Luther
(1520 letter to Pope Leo X)

"You see which is called the court of Rome, which neither you nor any man can deny to be more corrupt than any Babylon or Sodom, and quite, as I believe a lost, desperate, and hopeless impiety. This I have abominated and have felt indignant that the people of Christ should be cheated under your name and the pretext of the Church of Rome; so I resist."

Martin Luther
(1520 letter to Pope Leo X)

"When I started my newspaper humor column I was too old for a paper route, too young for social security, and too tired for an affair."

Erma Bombeck

"Better a witty fool than a foolish wit."

William Shakespeare

"It is my conviction that killing under the cloak of war is nothing but an act of murder."

Albert Einstein

"As the soul is dyed by thoughts, let no day pass without contact with the best literature of the world."

Sir William Osler, MD

"We build fine buildings and invent prodigious machines and pile up dazzling wealth. But the greatest of all human products is our knowledge."

Jonathan Rauch
(Kindly Inquisitors)

"I fear the Greeks, even when bringing gifts."

Virgil
(Aenid, II)

"O true believers, contract not an intimate friendship with any besides yourselves; they will not fail to corrupt you."

Mohammed
(Koran)

"We don't make the poor people rich by making the rich people poor."

President Abraham Lincoln

"We shall nobly save, or meanly lose, the last best hope of earth."

President Abraham Lincoln
(Speech to Congress, December 1, 1862)

"If it could be demonstrated that any complex organ existed, which could not have possibly have been formed by numerous, successive, slight modifications, my theory would absolutely break down."

Charles Darwin
(The Origin of the Species)

"Thanks to television, for the first time, the young are seeing history before it is censored by their elders."

Margaret Mead

"I consider promiscuity immoral. Not because sex is evil, but because sex is too good and too important."

Ayn Rand
(Playboy, March 1964)

"It ain't over 'til it's over."

Yogi Berra

"O true believers, take not the Jews or Christians for your friends; they are friends the one to the other; but who so among you taketh them for his friends, he is surely one of them."

Mohammed
(Koran)

"Thinking isn't agreeing or disagreeing. That's voting."

Robert Frost

"When the Man walked up he said,
'What is Wild Dog doing here?'
And the Woman said,
'His name is not Wild Dog anymore,

But the First Friend,
Because he will be our friend
For always and always and always.'"

Rudyard Kipling

"Follow the money."

Deep Throat
(Watergate Papers)

"All men are entitled to freedom of speech, freedom of worship, freedom from want and freedom from fear."

Franklin D. Roosevelt
(August 1941 Speech)

"The only limit to our realization of tomorrow will be our doubts of today. Let us move forward with strong and active faith."

Franklin D. Roosevelt
(April 1945 Speech)

"Whoever said there is no luck is wrong. You have luck when you are born in the United States of America with a sound body and mind and to parents who love and want you."

Larry O. Goldbeck, MD

"Seriousness is the only refuge of all ugliness."

Oscar Wilde

"Moderation is a fatal thing. Nothing succeeds like excess."

Oscar Wilde
(A Woman of No Importance)

"The Constitution gave the federal government no power to deal with common crimes, or to regulate individual conduct, or to take care of people in need. The Founding Fathers knew that politicians could use such power to reward their friends, punish their enemies, and gain control over your lives."

Harry Browne
(Why Government Doesn't Work)

"All the world's a stage, and all the men and women merely players. They have their exits and their entrances, and one man in his time plays many parts, his acts being seven ages."

William Shakespeare
(As You Like It, II-7)

"Don't' take 'no' for an answer. Never submit to failure."

Sir Winston Churchill

"Conservatives should be realistic enough to recognize that the United States is going deeper into socialism and will see expansions of federal power, whether Republicans or Democrats are in power."

Senator Barry Goldwater
(None Dare Call It Conspiracy)

"The soldier above all other people, prays for peace, for he must suffer and bear the deepest wounds and scars of war. But always in our ears ring the ominous words of Plato, the wisest of all philosophers, 'Only the dead have seen the last of war'".

Gen. Douglas MacArthur

"I always pass on good advice. It is the only thing to do with it. It is never any use to oneself."

Oscar Wilde
(An Ideal Husband)

"No creed must be accepted upon authority of a 'divine' nature. Religions must be put to the question. No moral dogma must be taken for granted—no standard of measurement deified. There is nothing inherently sacred about moral codes. Like wooden idols of long ago, they are the work of human hands, and what man has made, man can destroy."

Anton S. LaVey

Larry O. Goldbeck, M. D.

Henry Adams
John Adams
Louisa Mae Alcott
Woody Allen
Muhammad Ali
Maya Angelou
Susan B. Anthony
Mark Antony
Apostle John
Apostle Paul
Aristotle
Neil Armstrong
Marcus Aurelius
Francis Bacon
Roger Baldwin
Ian Barbour
James Barrie
Ethel Barrymore
Clara Barton
Bernard Baruch
David Bergland
Ingrid Bergman
Cardinal Joseph Bernardin
Yogi Berra
Ambrose Bierce
Josh Billings
William Blackstone
Elizabeth Blackwell, MD
Erma Bombeck
James Boswell
Louis D. Brandeis
Joyce Brothers
Harry Browne
Elizabeth Barrett Browning
Robert Browning
William Buckley, Jr.
Buddha
George Burns

Robert Burns
Edmund Burke
Leo Buscaglia
George W. Bush
N.M. Butler
Rhett Butler
George Gordon Byron
Julius Caesar
John Henry Cardinal-Newman
Thomas Carlyle
Dale Carnegie
George Washington Carver
Fidel Castro
Cervantes
Allan Chalmers
Cher
Winston Churchill
Cicero
Confucius
Joseph Conrad
Copernicus
Oliver Cromwell
Tony Curtis
Dalai Lama
Dante
Deep Throat
Daniel Dennett
René Descartes
Charles Dickens
Conan Doyle
Diogenes
Everett Dirksen
Walt Disney
Benjamin Disraeli
Amelia Earhart
Mary Baker Eddy
Albert Einstein

Dwight D. Eisenhower
Ralph Waldo Emerson
Medgar Evers
Adm. David Farragut
F. Scott Fitzgerald
Dr. Alexander Fleming
Ben Franklin
Milton Friedman
Erich Fromm
Henry Ford
Nathan Bedford Forest
Sigmund Freud
Robert Frost
J.W. Fulbright
R. Buckminster Fuller
Galileo Galilei
Mahatma Gandhi
Judy Garland
J. Paul Getty
Kahil Gibran
William Gladstone
Johann Goethe
Eugene O. Goldbeck
Larry O. Goldbeck
Oliver Goldsmith
Barry Goldwater
Edgar Guest
Nathan Hale
Dag Hammarskjold
Michael Hart
Victor Havel
Patrick Henry
George Herbert
W.E. Hickson
Sir Edmund Hillary
Adolf Hitler
Oliver Wendell Holmes

Homer
J. Edgar Hoover
Victor Hugo
Aldous Huxley
T.H. Huxley
Rep. Henry Hyde
Robert Ingersol
Holbrook Jackson
Jesse Jackson
Leon Jaworski
Thomas Jefferson
Jesus Christ
John Paul Jones
Carl G. Jung
Keats
Helen Keller
Walt Kelly
John F. Kennedy
Ken Keys
Omar Khayyam
Joyce Kilmer
Martin Luther King, Jr.
Stephen King
Rudyard Kipling
Henry Kissinger
James A. LaFond-Lewis
Ann Landers
R.D. Lang
Anton S. LaVey
Robert E. Lee
Lenin
G.E. Lessing
Abraham Lincoln
Walter Lippman
John Locke
Vince Lombardi
James R. Lowell

Martin Luther
Douglas MacArthur
Ernst Mach
Machiavelli
Naguio Mafouz
Norman Mailer
Nelson Mandela
Marcel Marceau
Groucho Marx
Karl Marx
W. Somerset Maugham
George McGovern
Margaret Mead
Mencius
H.L. Mencken
Michelangelo
John Stuart Mill
Edna St. Vincent Millay
Kenneth Miller
John Milton
Moliére
Christopher Morley
Moses
Benito Mussolini
Napoleon
Carry Nation
Isaac Newton
Florence Nightingale
Neitzsche
Richard M. Nixon
Sandra Day O'Connor
Scarlett O'Hara
Sir William Osler, MD
Ovid
Thomas Paine
Norman Vincent Peale
Harvey Penick

H. Ross Perot
Persius
Charles Pierce
Plato
Plutarch
Alexander Pope
Prier
William Proxmire
Rabelais
Ayn Rand
Jonathan Rauch
Ronald Reagan
David Ricardo
Eddie Rickenbacker
Will Rogers
Eleanor Roosevelt
Franklin D. Roosevelt
Theodore Roosevelt
Bertrand Russell
Jean Jacques Rousseau
Saint Jerome
Robert Schuller
Albert Schweitzer
Seneca
William Shakespeare
Ben Stein
Adlai Stevenson
Rene G. Torres
Andrei Sakharov
Leonardo da Vinci
Carl Sagan
Arthur Schopenhauer
Sir Walter Scott
Erich Segal
George B. Shaw
Tecumseh Sherman
Socrates

Gerry Spence
Spinoza
Josef Stalin
Barbara Streisand
Robert Louis Stevenson
Joseph Stillwell
Publilius Syrus
Mother Theresa
Helen Thomson
Henry David Thoreau
Alice B. Toklas
Arnold Toynbee
Spencer Tracy
William B. Travis
Harry S Truman
Mark Twain
Mao Tse Tung
Lao Tzu
Pope Urban II
Gore Vidal
Virgil
David Viscott
Voltaire
Wallis, Duchess of Windsor
Booker T. Washington
George Washington
John Wayne
John Wesley
Mae West
Oscar Wilde
Woodrow Wilson
P.G. Wodehouse
Frank Lloyd Wright
Adm. Isoruku Yamamoto
Y.B. Yeats
Henny Youngman
Emilliano Zapata

Larry O. Goldbeck, M. D.

About the Author

Larry O. Goldbeck, M.D., is an anesthesiologist. He did his medical specialty training at the University of Wisconsin following graduation from Baylor College of Medicine in Houston, Texas. He graduated with a chemistry degree from Baylor University where he played intercollegiate tennis. (He currently is a top thirty senior player nationally). He served during the Vietnam War and was recalled in the Naval Reserve for Operation Desert Storm in 1991. He retired as a Navy Captain in 1993.

Doctor Goldbeck is married to his college sweetheart, Nancy, and they enjoy their family fun with daughter Carol, son Glenn, and their four pre-teen grandchildren. Besides tennis he is active in travel, golf, and reading philosophy, religions, and history. For about ten years he has been a Libertarian and attends Mensa meetings regularly.

www.ingramcontent.com/pod-product-compliance
Lightning Source LLC
Chambersburg PA
CBHW030356290526
45785CB00004B/1775